TRIP TRAP

TRIP TRAP

JACK KEROUAC, ALBERT SAIJO & LEW WELCH

HAIKU ON THE ROAD

Edited by Donald Allen

CITY LIGHTS/GREY FOX • SAN FRANCISCO

Grateful acknowledgment is made to Ted Wilentz and Corinth
Books for permission to reprint several haiku which were first
published in *The Beat Scene.*

ISBN 10: 0-912516-04-6
ISBN 13: 978-0-912516-04-2
Library of Congress Catalog Card Number: 73-84120

Grey Fox is an imprint of City Lights Books.

Visit our website: www.citylights.com

CITY LIGHTS BOOKS are edited by Lawrence Ferlinghetti and
Nancy J. Peters and published at the City Lights Bookstore,
261 Columbus Avenue, San Francisco, CA 94133

CONTENTS

Editor's Note

By the time Albert Saijo wrote his excellent "A Recollection," with which we begin, both Jack Kerouac and Lew Welch were no more. Jack died of a massive hemorrhaging in October 1969, and in May of 1971 Lew Welch took his revolver and walked away into the forest of the Sierra Nevada foothills, never to be seen again.

But back in 1960, after the trip in the Jeepster Willy, Jack typed up the haiku he and Lew had jotted down in little notebooks and sent them to Lew. And Lew, inspired by Jack's demonstration of his technique of typing on a teletype roll, back home in Reno, sat down to write a novel, soon to be abandoned. "We Started for New York" is the opening section.

In July of 1960 Jack was back in San Francisco planning to take up Lawrence Ferlinghetti's invitation to stay at his cabin in Bixby Canyon down on the south coast. The following year he would write *Big Sur*, his account of that experience, in which Lew appears as "Dave Wain" and Albert as "George Baso."

The "manuscript of his notes, jotting, and texts on Buddhism" that Jack showed Albert (page 10) was published in 1998 by Viking as *Some of the Dharma*.

When Lew and Albert and Jack came to visit me at 38 Barrow Street in the Village, Lew told me of the BA thesis on Gertrude Stein he'd written for Reed College. In 1996 I published it as *How I Read Gertrude Stein*.

Donald Allen
September 1998

I SOMETIMES TALK TO
KEROUAC WHEN I DRIVE

Jack?

Yesterday I thought of something
I never had a chance to tell you
and now I don't know what it was

Remember?

                                    Lew Welch

Albert Saijo

A RECOLLECTION

People and things formerly present and vivid now dead or
forgot unless called to mind. Jack is dead. Lew is somehow
dead, or is it just that he wants us to think him dead? With
Jack there was his corpus. Lew simply disappeared. How
wonderful when you think of it! Perhaps we should all dis-
appear whithout a trace? Are you there, Lew? I have the
feeling you still appear among us from time to time in various
disguises. I sometimes believe you went into the mountains
that last time and had a truly illuminating experience. That
there in a pine-oak woodland or coniferous forest you reran
your life and came out ahead of it. That you then crossed
over the mountains and descended to the Great Basin where
you still are. Your hair has gone completely white but you
look younger in the face. You drink nothing but water. You eat
wild weeds, comb honey, and the fat larvae of the brine fly
that breeds in saline waters. You wear a faded blue chambray
shirt cut in cowboy style with small bone buttons set in silver
rims. You've got on faded gray Can't-Bust-Em trousers. You
wear basketball shoes without socks. You drive a faded green
Model-A coupe with wire spoke wheels and thin tires. You
have your final survival kit. You have a dog named Jim, a
border collie. You never raise your voice. You've been
appointed the sole agent and distributor of a certain power. It
is what you do. You're paid for it by check the first of each
month. Or, back in the mountains, you did actually blow out
your brain to metamorphose, and now your bones are falling
out of their sockets. In either case, you're no longer with us
as we are. This is about a time when you were still with us
alive in our way. Remember?

As I recall, it was rainy towards Thanksgiving when the
trip of *Trip Trap* happened. Both Lew and I were living at

Hyphen-House, a communal house on the northwest corner of Post and Buchanan in San Francisco. The house had just been organized at the time of these events. It was in a neighborhood half Black and half Japanese, with mostly Japanese shops and restaurants. Then there was Jimbo's Bop City around the corner that opened after hours, and nearby, Sullivan's Liquor Store that delivered both day and night. It was a busy neighborhood from early in the morning to very late at night. It was a noisy neighborhood. The area south of Post was being demolished. There were empty houses waiting to be torn down, left open without doors or windows, filled with human detritus, eerie to explore. And there were cleared off lots already taken by lush grasses, and weeds like brome, dandelion, common mallow, and filaree, with a few left-over stately trees, and drifts of trash. The whole area is on a broad incline facing southwest so that it was nice to look off over a clearing and see volumes of weather blowing in from the Pacific.

Hyphen-House was in a large wooden building painted battleship gray with a poolhall, shops, and restaurants at street level and five or six apartments in a row above. It had a balcony that ran along the front of the apartments at the second-story level overlooking Buchanan Street. We had the middle apartment. It was two storied with a commodious feel, especially downstairs where the ceiling was at least ten feet high. It might have been a prototype turn-of-the-century San Francisco two-story apartment. Logic was its strong point. It had gas-light jets.

We, that is Lew Welch, Les Thompson (through whom I came to know John Aubrey's *Brief Lives*), Tom Field, Philip Whalen, Jay Blaise and myself, moved into the place, cleaned it up and painted some. Then we furnished the place sparely from the secondhand stores of McAllister Street, with additional choice furnishings out of the abandoned houses close by. The outstanding piece of furniture in the house was the kitchen table. It was made of wood and had a top that could be expanded, and it had drawers, and under these regular drawers were bin drawers that rocked open. The kitchen was the social center of the house and this table was sat around a great deal for plain quiet talk or boozing and howling. It was before acid, there was occasional peyote and some grass. But it was mostly coffee, booze, and cigarettes. It was as Jack described it in the beautifully sustained prose of his book of suffering, *Big Sur*. I remember being kept indoors a lot by inclement weather. We led lives almost exclusively human.

Shortly after we moved into Hyphen-House we heard that Jack was coming to San Francisco from Hollywood where he had appeared on the Steve Allen Show. Then he was there, in the kitchen, seated at the table, with red plaid hunting cap set back on his head, and red check flannel shirt worn with tails out, and dress slacks with creases gone, knockabouts on his feet, looking downhome and French-Canadian. He was then at the height of his fame after *On the Road, The Subterraneans,* and *The Dharma Bums*. He looked tired and he was drinking heavy, but he appeared to be on a binge and determined to party on. He never lacked company. His celebrity drew company.

Earlier, Lew had gone to Reno to visit his mother. When he heard Jack was in town he came back. He was driving a Willys Jeepster, a present from his mother. He was proud of the car and called it Willy. Willy was written in the dust on the tailgate. Now the party had wheels and it bombed along from place to place till everyone fell down too tired or drunk to go on. The mornings after were deathly quiet. Jack would get up with a look in his eyes verging on the dead eye look of metabolic extremity and smile a ruined hungover smile. You understood then that his drinking was some kind of penance he had put on himself to do in a Mexican Indian Catholic way, and it brought to mind the 51st Psalm that begins, "Have mercy upon me, O God, according to thy lovingkindness . . ." Penance for what? God only knows, but why else did he do it? Sacrifice himself to juice. When he drank it was like he tore open his breast with his bare hands to show God his pure beating heart. So it went on till it was time to leave. Jack wanted to be back in New York for Thanksgiving. It was here Lew offered to drive him back in Willy. The trip was set. I decided to go along.

We started one rainy night from Chinatown with its colored lights reflected in the wet streets. First we had supper, then we looked through some shops so Jack could find a present for his mother. We drove then through the night and camped toward morning in the Mojave Desert for a few hours sleep. Our next stop was Las Vegas where we stayed in a motel designed after Washington's home at Mt. Vernon. We took in some of the dream state there. Looking off toward the mountains past the grandiose architecture of the casinos, Jack said, "Back in those hills are fellaheen waiting to come down." South to cement plug Hoover Dam then to 66. No time for Grand Canyon, alas.

Lew drove most of the trip. He drove with finesse, very much as he wrote. He had a light touch on the wheel, and he shifted his gears beautifully. He could double clutch. He had an even foot on the gas pedal, and his braking was soft. He heard his motor. Jack and I would take short turns at the wheel, but mostly it was Lew. I got the impression Jack didn't like to drive, it seemed to make him nervous. Willy ran fine, and from his snow tires, he had a deep hum as he rode. We were inside our microhabitat chamber sealed against the cold outside. We sped along. The country slipped by. We were provisioned with blankets and bags, spare tire, extra fuel, booze, peanut butter, bread, fig newtons, lettuce, jam, cigarettes, and milk.

There was diverse and sundry talk about politics and politicians, intricate crimes, talk of wars and panics, food, drink, clothes, beds, flowers, talk of women, relatives, home-towns, travel, foreign cities, talk about movies and movie stars, about sports and champions of sport, gossip of the literary life, ghost stories, fables, riddles, jokes, talk of grammar, of origins, about what's real and what isn't, and plain swap talk. Often a subject would develop from small beginnings and gradually be carried to lengths that outraged every normal expectation. Jack was good at doing this. Lew was good at spinning long tales. Then both Jack and Lew were into popular songs from the 40s. They both had fine singing

voices and good repertoires. Jack knew many Sinatra tunes
and could sing just like him. Lew was a great singer of scat.
So there were hundreds of miles of talk and song. There were
also long stretches of silence when we would each be deep
into our innermost privacies, or fallen into the very American
car trance where everything approaches in slow motion and
you become entirely curious and observant of the passing
landscape, noticing the conformation of the land, the flora
and fauna, marks of human culture, the weather, while at the
same time remaining perfectly aware of the car's relation to
the road. The moods a long car ride can put you through!

Buttes and mesas. Telephone poles whipping past. Small
towns. One such among some minor buttes, with bare cotton-
wood trees, a wooden water tank on a rise, board and batten
houses, quonset hut garage with old-fashioned gas pumps out
front, cars and trucks outside, people indoors. And so on
through Arizona, New Mexico, and across the short part of
north Texas and into Oklahoma where we turned northeast-
erly on a beeline for Indianapolis. We stayed in motels or
slept off the road in deserted places. Big steak in Texas and
fierce wind. In the middle of an empty plain where the pay
turnpike begins in Oklahoma a building straddles the highway
like a triumphal arch done after the manner of Holiday Inn.
Here I've lost confidence that it's a real place not a dream
place I've just described but let it stand. Reddish dusk. Then
into gentle wooded hills of southern Missouri. Crossed
Mississippi at St. Louis. Smell of coal smoke denoted that
west ended here and east began. Outskirts of East St. Louis, a
burlicue show in a low roadhouse. Enthusiastic performance
by girls in spite of small crowd. Snow falling in Illinois.
Stayed in a brick motel. At Indianapolis we had supper in a
bowling alley. Someplace between there and Columbus,
Ohio, camped in a wash, it was freezing cold, had a grand
bonfire. Got up at dawn. Even here Jack doing his brave daily
10 minute headstand. Now we were as well as in New York
City. Had only to cross narrow finger part of West Virginia
then Pennsylvania and New Jersey. Old hills and poor feeling
of coal country. In Pennsylvania drove through an old town

to find booze. Found one of the official state liquor stores, a clean storefront with no advertisements, inside spare and neat, Shaker fashion. Beautiful barns and small rolling hills of Pennsylvania. We approached Manhattan at night. Crossed New Jersey marshland and entered a bright tunnel and emerged into NYC and crossed town to dimlit Lower East Side corner bar from where Jack called Allen Ginsberg to say we had arrived.

New York is always a shock. A city based on small brutalities. A realm of total insanity, with its cruel hierarchies. We left the bar for Allen's place. We all felt rundown, but Jack wanted to do the town for several days before going home to Northport to rest. The Lower East Side is a slum. Allen lived around 2nd Street, as I recall. The street was thickly populated. Tenement houses on both sides of the street with tiny businesses tucked into the bottom of the buildings a step down from street level. Junk and garbage set out on the sidewalks. But the people were energetic, with alert, appraising eyes. We went up to Allen's apartment. The staircase and hallways of the building had a cavernous feel. Allen and Peter Orlovsky were home. Peter, who wrote true poetry like, "Thank god I have an innocent eye for nature." Lew presented Allen with a white wooden cross. He had taken it from the side of the road in Arizona, where crosses are placed at the site of fatal accidents. A ball of fluff that had fallen off a stripper's costume back in East St. Louis was attached to the cross. The cross was hung on the wall above the bed. There was talk. Peter explained to me that he'd been shitting rabbit pellets lately. He went to the bathroom and shitted a few and brought them to me in the palm of his hand. Sure enough, just like rabbit pellets. I saw St.-John Perse in the bookshelf. I was astonished by the volume of Allen's correspondence.

We went to Chinatown for supper in a brightly lit restaurant with marbletop tables and booths done in Chinese woodwork. It was a lively place. Allen spoke at table in a quiet, charming way, full of humor. Then after supper back into big city night. I never got over the feeling that Manhattan takes place inside a soundstage. Something about the narrow streets and low sky. A visit to a man named Huncke whose place was filled almost wall to wall with people laid out relaxing or stoned. Then to the apartment of the photographer, Fred McDarrah, where we put together the joint poem that appears in the book *The Beat Scene*. Later we took Jack to a couple of sisters (Fragility and Grace?) near Columbia University and left him there. Lew and I had no place to go. We had very little money. Drove down empty Wall Street. Rode Willy onto ferry and crossed to Staten Island then drove around the island looking for an out of the way place to crash. Drove off the road into a deserted lot and crashed among burdock. We woke to a cold, foggy morning and had breakfast in a railway car turned cafe all steamy warm inside. Crossed back over the water and ascended to the top of Empire State Building and looked over the solemn view. Then by chance we came into the use of an apartment. It was in the Village. Lent to us by a friend while she was to be with her mother out of the city. The apartment was in the shape of a U built around a light well.

We were with Jack most of the time. Went to the First Zen Institute for an evening service. The Buddha on the altar was offered marble cake and an orange, we were served marble cake and tea. The crowded Cedar Bar. Jam-packed Five Spot for Ornette Coleman. Saw Kirby Doyle. A loft in East Village with plants under skylight to see photographer named Frank. The painter Alfred Leslie, who had a large studio midtown for working on huge canvases. A visit with Don Allen in his quiet apartment with garden in back. Went to be with Jack while he was interviewed on the radio. Before the interview we were with the radio man at a small apartment he kept nearby the station for relaxing between his broadcasting chores. He was with his mistress. He had pills to keep him steady, and others to bring him up or ease him down. Then there were drinks. Enormous amounts of alcohol must be consumed daily in New York City. Lemming City, can there be a place more worldly?

Now we were fairly worn out. We crawled out of the city and made it to Northport, a quiet village facing the sound halfway out on Long Island. Jack lived here with his mother in a white cottage on a tree-lined street in a quiet neighborhood. The house was surrounded by a white wood picket fence. Jack's mother was Everymom. A stout, straightforward, friendly woman, whose feet hurt if she stood on them too long. Jack spoke mostly French with her. The relation between them seemed very clear and loving. She kept a neat clean house. There was a well loved cat. Jack asked his mother to cook a large supper for us.

He showed us the attic he'd converted to a studio where he did his writing. It had just been done and smelt new. In the middle of the room there was an electric typewriter on a small table with a simple straightback chair before it. It faced south through a window overlooking trees and the neighborhood. By a clever arrangement, a roll of teletype paper was fed into the typewriter so that Jack could type away at his ninety words a minute without having to stop every 11 inches to change paper. Next to the table was a standing lamp with a long flexible neck that had a bulb shaded with aluminum foil in a way to give him a small spot of light on the typewriter. He sat down to demonstrate. Being a whiz at it, when he typed he had no need to look down at the keyboard, he looked straight ahead. His fingers moved swift and sure over the keys. One could imagine him alone at night in this room, dark except for the small spot on his work, looking straight ahead and typing swiftly out of his mind. There were just a few books in the room, mostly different editions of his own work. He gave me a Japanese edition of *Subterraneans*. He showed us a manuscript of his notes, jottings, and texts on Buddhism. The extent of his study was quite impressive. I don't believe any part of this manuscript has ever been published.

Jack's mother put a wonderfully abundant supper before us. After, we sat in the parlor and watched television. When he was here at home, safe, relaxed, unharassed, the famous author bullshit set aside, you could see the great beauty and sweetness of his character. His mother went to sleep. He told us she had once worked in a shoe factory to support him. Now he could support her. To round out the evening he took us to a roadhouse by the side of an onion field. We had a few

drinks and did some hollering with the friendly locals, then
went back to the house and fell into the comfortable beds
Jack's mother had prepared for us.

Next day Lew and I went back to Manhattan. Before we left,
Jack took us out to the backyard with its well kept lawn, and
showed us where he had fallen over backwards with his vision
of Golden Eternity. He said he would see us in the city in a week
or so.

Back in the city, Lew and I did the place in relative
quiet. Museums. The caged animals in Central Park. Long
walks. Long subway ride deep into the Bronx. Walk over
Brooklyn Bridge for Hart Crane. A movie. Bookstores.
Coffeehouses. Visited friends from a former stay in New York.
I came to look forward to a drink about five o'clock each day.
Thanksgiving had come and gone, and I can't remember
where we spent Thanksgiving. Lew drove out to Northport
and brought Jack back into town. Carousing with Jack became
too sad to bear. A Middle Eastern cafe with belly dancers. A
Greek cafe with Greek dancing and resiny wine. Lew and I
decided to go back to San Francisco in time for Christmas.
We would also visit Lew's mother in Reno on the way. We
had come to the end of our string in New York. Jack spoke
of a trip to California the next year.

We took the shortest route to San Francisco. There was
a threat of snow through the Middle West. Lew drove in one
stretch to Indianapolis where we had a flat tire. From there
we drove in shifts. Gentle up and down over the low hills and
prairies of Illinois, Missouri, and Kansas. Bare trees, vast sky,
and ground with cover dead-back ready for winter. It was
cold and there weren't many people out. In Kansas stopped to
see a dead owl by the side of the road. We got out of the car
and knelt to the creature. The creature had a beautiful face, its
eyes on the front of its face like us. A sharp north wind ruffled
its breast feathers to show the fluffy down beneath. Golden
brown plumage.

Lew wasn't yet into the rough straits of his last years
with us. The years during which his harangues grew more
powerful and his anger poured from him like a virtual torrent

and he had that utterly fierce look in his eyes. He was calmer. This part of the trip was quieter than the part going east. It was a pleasure to be with him and listen to him talk. He told me his life story. I admired the style and precision of his natural speech. His great sense of the weight and motion of words, what he liked in Gertrude Stein. He could explain the most involved matters in small detail so that you clearly understood what he meant at all times. He showed an open, eager, boyish quality. He laughed relaxed. I'll never forget the beauty of his easy tears when he spoke of pathetic things.

We approached the Rockies and crossed over in a light snow fall and descended to Utah. Fishtailed over icy roads to the broad streets of Salt Lake City and on past the lake and through the desert to Bonneville Flats where we had breakfast in a cafe set against a bluff beside a sedgy marsh. Then into the endless panoramas of Nevada and its peculiar hamlets with their bright machines for gambling. In Reno, Lew's mother gave us a warm welcome. She took us to Chinese supper at a Polynesian restaurant. She gave us each five silver dollars to gamble. We strolled through several casinos playing slot machines. A light snow was falling. We lost all our money. The next day we drove out to Pyramid Lake and saw its tropical blue water and pyramid islands. The contrast between the white of the shore and the intense blue of the lake was striking. The day after, we did the last leg of our journey. We crossed over Donner Pass in a snowstorm and coasted down through the Great Valley and came to the bay at nightfall and drove over a lighted bridge to San Francisco where we parked Willy in the meager neon light of Buchanan Street. Up in the kitchen things appeared to be pretty much as they were when we left. But, of course, we know things are in a constant state of change. Hyphen-House was just another place from which all of us were to go elsewhere. The building itself is no longer there.

A NOTE ON THE TEXT. Lew must have had Gary's *Riprap* in mind when he called what follows *Trip Trap*. The text is mostly Lew, mostly his voice. Both Lew and Jack carried pocket notebooks, the kind spiral bound across the top, into which they jotted thoughts along the way. It was out of these notebooks that the joint poem "This Is What It's Called," which appeared in *The Beat Scene*, was written. *Trip Trap* must be out of the same notebooks, since it overlaps "This Is What It's Called" in many places. Lew, or Jack, appears to have done some polishing. For example, the long section on dirty assholes is more finished than the way it developed on the road. This particular conceit engaged us for several hundred miles. Here was an instance of a subject burgeoning outrageously from a small beginning. It wasn't based on any extravagant anality, but on the simple observation that people will walk around with shit on their assholes because it's hidden, but would never think of walking around with shit on their faces, though both face and asshole are part of the same body-temple. Somewhat the idea of the 'whited sepulchre' (Matt. 23:27). The section is also a lesson in commonsense proctological hygiene.

The section called "Masterpiece" is from Jack and Lew. I listened to them put it together.

The whole piece has the random quality of Brownian movement. It has the space of the hypnagogic state between waking and sleeping. It is offhand. It is a curiosity. It has a middle, but no beginning or end. It is neither interesting nor uninteresting, but it holds our attention somehow, for it appears to have an art after all, the fathomless art of random speech overheard through the course of a day.

May 1973

Lew Welch

WE STARTED FOR NEW YORK

We started for New York in my old jeep for no reason. No reason to stay in San Francisco, they fired me for eery reasons after saying I was doing just fine only that morning. That very morning when I came in with the piece of string through the hole in my ear I always wanted it pierced and finally did it, using as my excuse a huge costume party where you were supposed to come "elegant" and I had an old dress shirt bought in the good will by my girl — they get these dress shirts and boil them and don't put any starch in them so they come on all floppy, like Trelawny I thought, so I wanted to wear it and it needed the earring. A small gold one.

But word got around the Bemis Bag factory where I was starting to be a rubber-cutter (which is like cutting linoleum blocks, a real use for what we learned in the first grade). Most people don't know they print all the bags we use for every-thing by having big hand-cut plates of rubber, like linoleum blocks, it's cheaper, when you stop to think about the processes involved, to do the work, very intricate, by hand. And I liked it. Never having worked with my hands before. A very deli-cate extremely sharp knife and slow steady hands cutting out the patterns. A clean cut if you did it right, no little wobbles at all, tiny cliffs and gorges cut in the smooth gray rubber. Time went right on by. But they fired me.

One guy from some other part of the factory, at lunch, coming up to me and saying: "Ya hear about some nut in the cutting room getting his ear pierced? Who the hell was it?" And I said, "I don't know," with the string drooping out my ear, sorry I did it. And finally getting my check that afternoon with the explanation I'd come in late too often in the morning (which was true), and "And . . . no, that's the only reason." He was embarrassed.

I was hurt but free. And rich. Two pay checks all at once. But discouraged and angry, I liked the job, and was sitting around pouting and thinking how I needed my girl to say, "There there Lewy" (which she never naturally said, it was only a little joke between us — kidding on the square). When the phone rang and I learned Jack Duluoz was in town and wanted me to come over. And I went over to see my girl and talked so much and so furiously she couldn't have worked "There there Lewy" into it even if it was the sort of thing she could, naturally, have done. And met Jack Duluoz and was drunk for 3 days.

The costume party was a big flop. I came on with the damned earring and the floppy poet-shirt and a sash, but it wasn't "elegant" because I drank too much rum and got sick, pot-sick, mixing them. And my girl who was very elegant in a flapper sort of way for the party got disgusted and wouldn't let me in her apartment. "I've got my own life to live, you know," she said and for some reason it meant everthing horrible and not-love, and I deeply loved her. So I walked away again. I do that. I just walk completely away and never come back. It just didn't seem like there was any hope of making anything really happen to happen, it was really over though the incident was trivial and I didn't want to come into her apartment that night anyway.

Then Jack and I and Prosmo Kantner, the painter, sat on the hillside of Twin Peaks and looked at the bay and drank 3 quarts of Pernod, hot. All afternoon. And two little kids came up and I was playing the Red Monk in half-lotus position staring at the beautiful bridge and bay. Jack said to the kids, "He's a real monk sitting there. He can make things happen." And I tried to make a horse down the hill lift his head and switch his tail. The horse did, finally, but the kid was unimpressed. He said, "My mother taught me to sit like that," and sat in a full lotus easily with his limber little bones, and then he said, "That's my horse. We used to have another one but one day my grandfather went out to feed it and the horse reared up and kicked him in the head and he died. So then we got this other horse."

There wasn't any reason for staying in San Francisco and Jack wanted to drive across the country again, so I said all right we'll leave after Thanksgiving because the girls want to cook us a big dinner. We cook the turkeys and they cook the pies. But the night before they all got drunk and Valerie Song threw a half-full gallon bottle of port at point-blank range to crash and break full in the face of Jay Blaise who'd been needling her. That did it. Violence is sickening and silly. And everything else had gone wrong for a whole week. It didn't put Jay's eye out but it wasn't her fault. And wouldn't apologize — found herself backed into a corner of ego-helpless shame and clinging to her little hang-ups saying (but not really meaning it), icy: "Oh, I didn't put out your eye? Too bad. "

So we decided to leave right away, missing Thanksgiving, and called Albert over from Mill Valley. It was a ruined schedule for Albert: he'd wanted to go to the bank in Chinatown and get his money out. But he wasn't fazed. He just packed everything in his little carton for mailing home laundry when you're in college — his survival kit: a few clean clothes in a laundry box. And it was evening of the next day after the Broken Port Bottle and Jay gave us each a charm: Jack got a St. Christopher medal, I got a Jewish coin with a lion and the ten commandments, and Albert got a Mexican penny. So we said to everybody, "Goodbye goodbye," revving the jeep up and went to Chinatown for a last meal and took off into the night — driving across the bridge with SF "the smallest city in the world," my home, looking like a single lit hill.

It's a jeep station wagon which I set up with a mattress in the back for long trips. Extra gas can with 2 gallons in it. One new tire. A cracked windshield. And the engine already throwing oil very badly. It worried me, but I figured Willy would make, as he did, beautifully.

No point in telling everything. Finally getting to the part about the cross and the whore-candy. But you have to know it was magical all the way. Not that occult nonsense, but the actual magic that happens if we'd but see — and when we see it, not strange at all. Drunk or sober, high or not, the magic little ways of this planet going on mostly unnoticed by all us worried humans. But on this trip we noticed and knew and were calmed by it. It was probably because of Albert and Jack and the oil-spurting car and no reason and our love for each other and the land we drove across and fatigue. Fatigue will always help it. You're too tired not to notice.

First we slept in the Mojave desert and woke up to oranges Albert had brought along. Then Jack wanted to take a little run to get the stiffness out (first night sleeping in Willy, too small, and no water to wash your face and later, maybe 11:00 in the morning, than we'd planned). We were on this little road out into the desert so the highway seemed far away and very small. And we jogged along like fighters up the little side road, away from the highway, running straight into that flat dry nothing of Mojave, and Jack said: "I wrote this 3 years ago. I always wondered what it meant."

Three men running up the road. The wrong direction.

And we started talking to the fourth guy. We'd turn around, all of us in the front seat talking, and one of us would turn around and start to say something to the empty back of the jeep. Or we'd hunt for 4 chairs in a restaurant. We all did this. We never knew who he was. But he was male and very gentle and he got out somewhere in Oklahoma.

So, finally, the cross.

We were driving across Arizona and the highway has crosses beside it wherever somebody's been killed in cars. They have big crosses for adults and little crosses for children. Sometimes a whole cluster where a family got wiped out. It really got to you, finally. Highways are very dangerous places.

Gradually we all decided to steal a cross. I don't know why. At first we thought we'd put it on the grill of the car, like deer horns, but then we knew that wasn't very prudent. So we were slamming along about 70 miles an hour, at sunset, and I saw this single cross. A long straight stretch of road and nobody coming. It took a long time to slow the jeep down, being in overdrive, so we were about a hundred yards away from the cross when I got out. I started running up the road, in the West, the country rolling gently with sage and the sunset very beautiful and low against the sky — right along the bottom and murky. I thought "I'll bet I can see the little cross against the sunset" so I stooped down, still running, only now all stooped like Groucho Marx. Finally I stopped, because I still couldn't see the cross. I got way down. I had to kneel to see it. I knelt and saw the cross against the sunset and found I was kneeling in thorns.

It was wooden, painted white, with the pointy bottom covered with red Arizona dirt.

Three of us in a Jeep with a white cross 80 miles an hour now, trying to get there. Albert sitting very quietly in the back, looking at everything go by — his first transcontinental driving trip. Jack and I yakking, solving all the problems of the universe all over again, passing the port bottle back and forth. Then every once in a while saying "Albert, what've you been seeing all this time?" And Albert would say: "I just saw the strangest thing. A white horse standing in an abandoned store front." He sat sideways on the mattress, looking out the windows.

————

Albert Saijo fought with the Nisei troops in Italy. He wouldn't cut his hair. He and his whole family were sent to the concentration camps America sent Japs to during the war. They went to Wyoming and lived in tarpaper shacks and lost all their property in California because they were Japanese and America was fighting the Japanese. Albert was only 16 and later said he liked the camp. When he was 18 they drafted him and he fought in Italy. In Italy he never cut his hair and spent most of his time with Hawaiians who were very tough. He was thin because of his T.B. and never cut his hair no matter what they threatened to do, and was very tough.

One night, on pass, he was accosted by a 10-year-old Italian boy with the same story: "Want a piece of ass, Joe?" and said, "O.K." The boy led him to a building that was all bombed out on the bottom floor. The bottom floor was all gone except for a wall here and there and a staircase leading up to the second floor which, miraculously, was still intact. The boy led Albert up the stairs and into a room where two women, one about 50 years old and one 12 years old, were eating something at a table with a candle on it.

The 12 year old girl, who was very beautiful, got up and led him into the next room.

"When I kissed her," Albert said, "I tasted milk."

TRIP

TRAP

HAIK

E'en lions look
    at me

ALBERT'S HAIK

I like to sleep
    in little snatches

Lost Davis

HAIK

The national hair
            scalp
                oil

LEW

The music of
    her little ear
        was trembling
        in my fly

The lorn are rude

LEW

Old men drive slowly
backwards
    in Safeway Parking Lots

LEW

The torn eat food

Movie Heat

Albert Saijo
working out an old
    Burmese Karma

Angel pussy—
"Would you care to
  stick your cock
    in my halo?"

Samsara comes
from Nirvana

LEW

On a disappearing road,
    among crenelated mtns.,
Thinking of whores

C O M M E R C I A L S

(1)   Girl eating soup
(2)   Polaroid Buddha
(3)   Gumluv Family
      Style Puce
      weird huge brush
      mouth full of
            shit
(4)   Planked
      muscalunge

The whole world
must become
    crazy because
    we dont want
        anyone to arrest
        anybody anymore

LEO'S APHORISM

All is Free
When Law is Not

I have dissolved
   the bean
under my tongue
(and then say
      no more)

Goodyear Snow Tires
   Xtra Grip
(rear tires, new
   jeep, green
   dharma wagon
   color)

Atlan Grip

LEW

Absolute stone turds
   shit by huge
      stone turds

LEW'S HAIK

I want
 a big wet fuck
 in Winslow

LEW'S HAIKU

On the golden hills
  the fat live oaks
Browse like Buffalo

You're surrounded by
    buildings that used to
            have

A thousand people
    working in them
    —that's *good*

It would be good to
    be sleeping
    in Joplin

Sign in Amarillo
  T h i s   D o o r

LEW

I dont care what
    it is myself,
Texas or third base

The trees, already
    bent in the windless
Oklahoma plain

Albert in the old
    outhouse: "Years
And years of shit
            in there"

Picasso is watching
    the children
     of the world
    move beneath
    his Riviera nuggets

LEW'S HAIK

We are flake off of
        All-Sun
                (as Crane said
                "harnessed jelly
                of the stars")

We slouch in slouch thot
Surviving across the
                    U.S.A.
    75 miles an hour
            through slouch towns
            ranges and sticky swamps

LEW

This is not germane
    to your course,
Doctor Blair

ALBERT

Dick Deadwood
        rides
    a shortlegged
        Mongolian pony

"Hey look, a
        red road"

"The road's been
    red a long time"

Big steaks of honey——
Big snakes of honey——

Talking Albums Blowing Sessions:
should be called "TRIPS"

Eating nectar from
    the flowers, bees
Shit honey

A: Honey is bee shit

J: Is it really?

A: Yes, the bees back
    into those little holes
    and shit!

J: What do they eat to make honey
            like that?

A: Flowers

L: The Nectar of the flowers

A: That's what you call a Playtex

LOOKING AT LEW'S FLASHLIGHT

Those Boy Scouts
  are smart fuckers
For such little kids

There's a hole
in the Island

"What is the Indian
  saying around here?"

"There are none
  around here."

I pledge to my
customers as a
Texaco Dealer
that my *registered*
bathroom shall
always be clean
and fully equipped—
     Isnt that sick?

Gregory and Allen
　　and Peter
make up
　　their poetry
　　out of insanity
　　& Lower East Side

ALBERT

Grain elevators on
　　Saturday lonely as
Abandoned toys

LEW'S ALTERNATE

Lonely grain elevators
　　on Saturday
—Abandoned toys

JACK'S ALTERNATE

Grain elevators on
　　Saturday waiting for
The farmers to come home

Windmills in Oklahoma
—What shall I
Liken thee to?

The windmills of
  Oklahoma look
In every direction

Radio antennas in
      Texas are hard to see,
Said the cow

When a cow is puking
      in Oklahoma,
A cow is resting in Nebraska

Those two tanks
      are there
On the highway
  —Hockey pucks

To call them tanks
is mere speculation

'Course you know
what Greta Garbo
    would say: —
        Tanks

A guy I played
 pool with
   said "I'll kill
   the motherfucker
    says I dont love
    e v e r y b o d y "

LEW

A coral colored Cadillac
        in Texas
Threw gravel all over us,
        our beat jeep
        —Our windshield is nicked
            but our eyes
            are
        C L E A R

LEW

Cadillacs are always in a hurry
  Call it a watchpocket book
    Look at these buildings
    What are they DOING here
    This arroyo & that sand
    I last saw Amarillo
      as a soldier
      smoking my first cigar
      & Roosevelt
        died

Roosevelt
  had a dirty asshole
  so we had
        Pearl Harbor
Hitler had a dirty ass
so we had Buchenwald
Senator McCarthy
    had a dirty asshole
    & he died
Not one cowboy
    in Texas
    has a clean asshole
    But there is one
      in Las Vegas
Alexander Pope
had a dirty asshole
T S Eliot prays for
    the dirty asshole
T S Eliot's fog
  had a dirty asshole

The last time I saw Paris
   I had a dirty asshole
Pres Eisenhower
      plays golf
      with a dirty asshole
No insult intended to
      his partner
   All we mean is,
wash your asshole
after you shit,
with water, clean,
   & you'll feel good
      & clean
Bishop Sheean's
   wild look
comes from a dirty
      asshole
Everybody in America
is walking around
with a dirty asshole
A little bit of water
      goes a long way
All of Stendhal
   can be understood
All of Stendhal
      results
From a dirty asshole.
Santa Claus
   has a dirty asshole
Philip Lamantia
   could be taught
   to cleanse his asshole
I have no hope
   for the Senators
   or the Senatrix
Nor was Cleopatra clean
   Nor Vercingetorix

No Roman pickaninny
  outhoused wide.
Thou cleaneth
where food entereth
Why not attend the port
  of the leavings
All holes in the body
Shd be clean with water
  All holes baptized
  Holily
  Holy like li li lock
    All holes shd be baptized
      because all holes are holy
              I am tired
              of this talk of holes
              For holes is where
                    my skin
                      is not
"Shit, Snyder,
  you know what
    they do in
    those monasteries
    —you'll come back
      with your asshole
          stretched
        the size
        of a wagon
            tire"
        said Rexroth

Thats a beautiful poem
—I mean fire
I am not bounded
by this bag of skin
nor bones skew me
    "I love Jesus"
    says the sign
    Are we still on holes?
Let our assholes be clean
    as the hole in the donut.
As the doors to our temple
Which sports
    One turning shoe
The asshole of Dixie
        is dirty
    Dixie has a dirty asshole
        Dulles died
        with a dirty asshole
        & went to Heaven
            though
            (innocent)
And I saw
    a great vision
    of Little Orphan Annie
    eyes sightless as an asshole
        MacArthur returned
        to Manila
        with a dirty asshole
Hirohito rides his
            white
            horse
    with a dirty asshole
Hirohito's white horse
    has a dirty asshole
        Napoleon on Elba
            not clean

The final asshole line
    is
        Wash Thyself
We shoulda got
    Shirley Temple
        in there
Oh the man
    that arrests us
Will have
    a dirty asshole
That's an endless thing
Let's talk about shacks in Texas
    And the birds
        on seaweed
            wheat
                plains

Fences

Cars beetle over & rust
        in Texas (Albert said)

Texas Continues

Takes two to con
———go

There is a cross
    imbededded
There is a hell
    imbedded in this earth
    like a cross
    in a Arizona highway

Believe me,
Dont drink when
you're plastered

Whore candy

I made a mistake
        but. . . .I got out
                    of
                    it

A herd of browsing
                cattle
One calf runs

There's Mister I-Cower-
    under-My-Car

Some guys go around
jingling like slaves
of Santa Claus
with dingleberries
which are little
    hard balls of dried shit
    encrusted on asshole hairs

Pigtailed sisters
& baldheaded fathers

The various Joplin
    ordinances
Hincty, burn
    your brights

Nor tell the tolling road
    go lone

Yum Yum

A thousand books on
        Indians—they all
look alike, the anthropologists

They cheat people
with these old
cigars!—the
only person that
   didnt cheat is
   Robert Burns

LEW'S HAIKU

I turned into
      a gas station
—The engine stopped

In the desert
   sun, a yellow
Caboose

ALBERT

Seems like stealing
      candy
from a baby,
      this road

The new moon
        is
the toenail of God

LEW

Two empty buildings
Windmill Nevada
Everybody went away
The town still stays

Leo driving
    thru the West
    with his cock
        of port,
        passing trains

Sign in Arizona

DINAH DOESNT

Ten-ounce K.C. steaks
    with ice-cold water
On the wrist (Albert)

Good french frieds,
     everything good

The honey farts—
    this nasty machine

Green & silver signs
  in New Mexico
  say Refinery Exit
    One Mile

They make good coffee
  in Oklahoma

Asking Albert for
a poem, he said
     nothing

Mormon popflops
  among silos

"I dont like pussy jam,
     it tastes funny"
          —GUY IN CHICAGO

CLAUDE'S HAIKU

     Ah the moon
     —I see it
     In the wine I spilled

JACK

Grain elevators
     are tall trucks
     that let the road
          approach them

HAIKU FOR ALFRED LESLIE

Gagging
     on Old Smuggler
     on an endless Texas

Silly old fool
blowing a long toot
  towards Juarez

ALBERT

It's us humans
  give things
Back and front

JACK & LEW

Mormons who had
narrow little wagons
  have left us
  very wide streets
        and
          temples
          with
          no
            nails

LEW

I always take
          more keen,
I cook it in a rifle
      and shoot myself

ALBERT
FUCKING WITH THE MUSE IN TEXAS

The country is blond
    and flat.
For fifty miles
couldn't think
of anything but that whore
in Chicago and the tub
            of oysters

LEW

Edible grain
    with snow on it

"Look at the fucking size
    of that fat star"

"That's a light"

They have the
    funniest pillows
In motels

These arent pillows,
they're fucking
assholes

The sons of Zaddock
move on

No Health Allowed
by Order of
STATE PET
Department


```
*  *  *  *  *  *
 *  *  *  *  *
  *  *  *  *
   *  *  *
    *  *
     *
```

MASTERPIECE

The Lion said "I
   demand too much"
and walked up to the Zebra
and said I want to eat you
   The Zebra ran away
and the Lion chased him
   & want Pa-Wow
   & ate the Zebra anyhow

And the Vulture said
   Vuuuuuuuuuu
"Oh look what the Lion left
   Slurp slurp"
   Then the ants & the worms
      came
"Look what the Vulture left"
And then the sun came
   & said "Look
      what the worms & ants left'

And then there was dust
And then came the sun
And then came eternity
   & said "Oooh look
      what the sun left"
And then came the Lion
   & said "Look
    what eternity left—
    I think I'll make
    a little world here."

RED MONK'S COMMENTARY

The lion áte the zebra
And the zebra ate the lion
And the lion was eternalized

****

****

It's all arranged to come out even
If only people werent so hincty
They try to make it work
to someone's advantage

—

In New Mexico
    there is a place
    called Iyanbito
    and a sign
    that says Exit
    —then there is
        a sign that says
        Keep off Median

LEW

Used to walk around
singing "Silent Night"
in the Bemis Bag Factory
in October

Think of it—
    a whole lifetime—
        not one mistake—
            —ANONYMOUS JAPANESE

The boy looks
His father does not see
The boy will look
Or learn he must not see

ALBERT

In Texas
   Leo's cock
   turned to glass
   and he wrapt it
     in gold foil

In Oklahoma darktown
He put 30¢ in
   and dragged out a 25¢
   packa cigarettes
     aint that a stupid
      thing to do, to be
     a healthy lad
     turning a cafe barstool
      at 8?

Well
     Carrots

Little hands
   lay largest gifts

Death————
    sleeping in the woods
    with a fucking
    blanket of earth

My theory
    of driving
       is
to let people
        sleep—
I never hit
    the brake
       or the gas jet
         hard

The description
of one Kalpa cowflop

Senzaki was a waif
    in Mongolia
A Mongolian Waif

Indiana——white horse
   standing in
An abandoned storefront

She wants to learn
  what we know
But she's too nervous

Emergency oil
  Emergency gas
    I'll tell the world
    To kiss my ass
                    (Lew)

And then I ate
the cheese
With Jack Kerouac
& tasted Carroway
    Seeds

KOKELL THE PLUMBER SAID
IN NEW YORK WHEN WE GOT THERE

——My theory
        is I burn
I burn a lot
        If it's not there
It's not there

                    F I N I

Letters to Jack Kerouac in Northport
from Lew Welch in Reno, 1959–1960

Crispness Day 1959

Dear Jack,

So here we are in Reno where Sweet Willy brought us
through a beautiful snowstorm in the Rockies — small dry
flakes blowing horizontal over small pines and huge gorges
of red rock. We stopped just below the summit and had a
terrific snowball fight which left my heart pounding so loud
I couldn't hear the snow fall (Albert claimed he could) the
whole world white and silent and the two of us motionless
listening while Willy steamed.
    We really pounded 800 miles a day, slept once in a
bitter cold little wayside park in Indiana, hoar frost on the
neatly cut grass and a wild outhouse with a ceramic urinal
like an empty birdbath. It was cold. Both sleeping on the
mattress and discovering Albert is a mattress thief (I had only
one foot for my bones) and I am a blanket thief (he finally
jammed a corner of the sleepybag under an elbow) and we
both shivvered and dint sleep. In Ohio I saw and said:

        A lone hound loping across grass with
        Hoar frost on it in Ohio
        Sniffing cows

Lots of things, but two very strange ones: we burnt out the igni-
tion switch after driving through a very beautiful fog — so thick
you couldn't see more than 100 feet in a circle around while
slamming over a straight highway 75 miles an hour — a blasting
little circle of speed in a white light crashing straight into the void
ahead (it could, really, have dropped right off at the edge of sight)
— and when the fog hit the bushes in the desert it instantly froze
so it was like driving through sparkling coral, purity-white, in
a white ring of light thrown down by some unbelievable
spotlight way way up the Universe — little green Willy in the
moving center. Then, incredibly, we broke through into a perfect
hot summer desert day. No clouds. Hot sun. Landscape went
hundreds of miles in all directions and ended with purewhite

mountains. So we stopped to look and breathe and piss in the patchy snow and red ground and then got back in the car and found it wouldn't work. No nothing. No gauges working when the key was turned. So I filled it with gas from the survival can and rolled downhill trying to start it, but it was clearly a broken car that would never run again and LO! There ahead where you'd never dream it was a gang of men surveying. I fiddled and fussed and then went over very cool, cool as a hill-billy, and like Rupe I told you about, made it their problem. I just stood helpless and waited. Finally a great hero with a small mustache (who was writing down the figures as the others with tripod and tape called out incomprehensible numbers) and he ambles over and asked a few questions and then said "you gotta hotwire it." So he was prolly a Neal-like guy who stole cars and knew how to get by the ignition switch, you just yank all the wires out and wind them all together and the car works without key. So the strange thing is this tragedy occurred within 100 yards of the only humans on the road for 200 miles in blank Nevada. We roared on.

Strange thing 2: we got here at Mom's home just as she was leaving the house. She'd been here only 10 minutes after returning from a long trip to SF and the Doctor. If we got there 10 minutes earlier or later there'd be nothing but a blank forbidding house and us with $6 left, no gas, and tired.

Strange thing 2a: In NY we wanted to leave Friday but I got a huge foreboding feeling — really evil — so bad I couldn't sleep and said "Albert, we can't leave today or tonite something awful will happen" and Albert said "Is that so?" and so we didn't. If we had: empty house, no money, tragic night, worry, confusion, Mom's Xmas ruined, etc. (+ maybe huge truck running us down in Utah, who knows?)

But the strangest thing of all was earlier, when I was fired in SF. It happened exactly when you arrived as if to make it necessary I should know you and drive you back and so forth. I mean it. The boss was very confused, like he didn't know why he had to let me go. And I was hurt and confused. But then for months I had this strange sensation of being in a scene that was wrong, where I was only marking time, nothing happening, getting lazy, wrong girl, and so and so and so.

"It is hard being born to the Dharma, now in America. We're real pioneers" (remember Albert saying this?)

But we finally get to this ununderstandable condition where it's clear we're floating along somewhere close to the actual spinning of the all-wheel, working, I'm absolutely convincingly convinced, slowly toward the ultimate hub, the great WHEE, survival-center. How strange! How bizarre!!

And we ain't doin' NOTHING!!

I have all these warm things I want to say to you my greatest real friend since Gary and Whalen and, lately, Albert. How to say it in homosexual America where to love a friend is despised and ridiculed, but you know this. And I worry about how, despite your admonitions, you might have been hurt and troubled by my Leo-eating of Lois — which dint mean anything but I was so hungry, nothing but bad sex, worse love, for 3 years, and finally this great graceful unreluctant Lehmbruck of a girl. YUM! YUM!!

But I worry that my hungriness might have hurt you who I love far more, so I've taken a huge vow of celibacy — I mean it

For years I've chased cunt till I dropped, found good and bad, ended up with about 2 real good months a year, all the rest wasted and worried (I've never been a real cocksman, always fell in love). I've hurt and been hurt, and IT AIN'T WORTH IT — all america I see killing itself for something you only need twice a week — and all the SHIT THAT GOES WITH IT!

I quit (hopefully Gavin Arthur's 60 year + statement that only after announcing celibacy did the ladies really get down to business and lay him).

Sigh.

But I mean it, the love. I worry about all those "squint-eyes" hating you for books that are only truly written about plain people doing what they do, written from your great compassion, not one hurting police-word or snigger (as the bright-boys do). You mustn't let them hurt you as much as they do. Remember to say (like Christ) "poor babies." They really don't know what they do. They really have no viciousness. Only fear. They don't hate us, they only fear us who have no fear. And no hate can come without fear. And fear cranked high enough, becomes hate. But only innocent.

We must wait, as the sutras say, until the very last sentient being is totally enlightened. It will take endless kalpas of kalpas. Meanwhile we say: "sure, I'll come back, why not?"

It is boring being all light. So we come back. Get thrown down, and back, willingly. Watch a baby, if you get a chance, coming out into this world. He WANTS to be born. The worst way. Which is what happens. For, to be a human, mostly light, is worse than being a cranberry plant. Less light he has, but still spends all his soul reaching for Sun. As we do, but we KNOW it, and yearn.

Albert and I did our wash today and read *Maggie Cassidy*. Me for the second time. What happens is I drop right into it. You must forget all this and WRITE!

You, Allen, and Corso are the great scab-rippers. Writing was all scabbed over. Now it flows and scares everybody. But what a huge achievement! Maybe a better image would be a river all iced over — but it waren't no THAW! It was ripped out of all despair and pure knowledge you just have to write out of all that love simply. Good.

Albert is reading *Alice in Wonderland*. Mom is cooking and talking about how she'll die when she's 100 and won't leave me anything — kidding. I am writing this letter.

You should have been with us on that trip — beautiful. Go route 40. More mountains. Etc.

I got a new survival hat for Christmas. A real Basque beret. It comes over both eyes and ears for blizzards. Rest of the time, jaunty.

Merry Christmas to you and Memere (spelled right?). I think, if at all, about Rogue River. Prepare yr. survival kit. Have faith.

Love,

Lew

5 January 1960

Dear Jack,

This is my new teletype roll.
It is white.
I like it.
It is truly endless.
Only I have it on the floor and when I write along
there's too much tension and I have to unroll a little bit of it,
let it have some room, loosely hanging there, or it gets dug
into by little barbs on this machine, but that is all right.

I'm here in Reno at last after some very tiresome times
in S.F. Everybody is sulking or flipping. Except Philip, who
always does just fine these days. And Albert, who says: "Is
that so?"

Yesterday I wrote poetry because the night before I had a
huge message from my Muselady, to wit:

> First you must love your body, in games,
> in wild places, in bodies of others
>
> Then you must enter the world of men and
> learn all worldly ways. You must sicken.
>
> Then you must return to your mother and
> notice how quiet the house is
>
> Then return to the World that is not Man
>
> That, finally, you may walk in the world
> of men, speaking

All day today I wrote on my novel and got all hung up.
It is hard for me to start . . . the point of my title "Hard Start."
There is definitely something wrong with writing a long con-
tinuous thing on small, discontinuous, pieces of paper.
Tomorrow I scrap everything and start again on this huge roll,

and I promise not to turn it back for reading and worrying until miles have been done.

It is absolutely quiet here, all day long. The dog sleeps under old bathrobes. I wash dishes and bake hams. I have been depressed and have a cold, but now am coming out of both these illnesses.

Haselwood is printing Whalen's book beautifully. About Feb. 15 or so he'll do my best poem *Wobbly Rock*, a long 6 part thing, as a broadside with illustrations and fine calligraphy.

My mother sends best wishes to you and your mother, and I do too-.

Lew

"Whatya doin' sittin' there with your hat on? well, I guess that's a pretty good idea anyway when you have a cold you oughta keep your head warm"

The hat is my real Basque beret, now my survival-writing hat, and that was my mother speaking as usual without periods or pauses.

Since I started using this teletype roll I drop right into this book whenever I start. Only, mystically, I can't seem to get back into it now that I have cut off the section I was writing, which I did in order to write several letters. What I am going to do is scotch tape the thing back together as soon as I finish this note. Surely it will all start flowing again.

The time is midnight. I took a nap, feel fresh, and intend to pound away far into the night.

So far the book is very funny (to me). I sit here and chuckle and roar and am very surprised at the antics of Leo Keeler and his funny friends. I have about 30 feet done. I intend to do another 10 or 15 feet tonight.

This is the first time I have really lived like a writer. Stein used to say that writing was a matter of working only a few hours a day "I myself write only a half-hour a day and it's surprising how much writing gets written in only half an hour a day day after day, but of course I wait around all day for that half hour." She is very wise. That is what I do. I wait around, and then find myself at it again. No pain at all. I drop right in and *wham* that ol' book keeps writing away at itself (I have very little to do with it — prolly the real writer is some lunatic Zen monk down here inside me for kicks). Then I stop and drink some Burgundy (the best wine for writing — port is much too powerful for me — I get sleepy), and off I go again, and then finally I'm not doing it anymore, I'm out in the backyard, taking a walk, or reading a book.

I don't know how to thank you for telling me about this teletype roll, and about living with your mother. Also, by direct mind transmission you gave me that more important thing that no one else has given to me — some mysterious total take about how, if you are going to be a writer, you must sit down and write and write. Everybody says this but you *transmitted it* to me. Thank you. Writing is just fine. It really is a fine thing to do. And all the rest is chatter.

Now naturally I was a writer before this, but not totally and with no other thing going on. Other things, of course, are going on but they are now going on in a writer — where before they were the little hectic things that kept making me nervous and making me wonder "when do I get time to write?" Of course you don't get time to write, you write.

I got your card. It is nice to think that LoLoLoLee (as I call her in my delighted memory) I say: "Hello LoLoLoLee," it is nice to know that she remembers and really likes me. Also your plan about long sea walks and quiet months is good. You must write about "The Whole United States" at once — I told Larry Ferlinghetti about that title and he flipped — said I should use it myself, but we always already discussed about how L.F. looks at ideas as if they were rare things one must save and steal and not just throw out and share. The trouble is he really isn't sure there is plenty more where that came from — the void, the empty unfillable void where nothing is *so perfect*, etc. and on.

I have a lot to say, but must stop this and get back to work.

One thing though. Going through my things and helping my mother go through hers has convinced me that the Survival Kit idea is absolutely essential and should reduce itself as follows:

> 1) a pack with sleeping bag basic equipment (as per any 5 day camping trip, including food) which must weigh less than 50 lbs — preferably less than 40.
> later we must compare notes, then send our final list to Roshi Snyder for approval and corrections. But not now.
> 2) (and here is my new idea) typewriter, paper, manuscripts, city-survival equipment such as a

sportcoat and maybe a pretty pair of pants and a
pretty shirt, etc. etc. can ALL be put into a
FOOTLOCKER

3) books etc. etc. must be stored at the home of
one's mother, or at the home of a friend near the
SURVIVALEE'S favored part of the world.

Of course, the footlocker can be pretty much of a drag unless
you have a car, but I am completely convinced that a survival
kit must include a car (for me, anyway) and that that car must
be a Jeep station wagon. Those who wish to survive and who
(like you) do not wish to have a car, can easily handle the
footlocker on buses, trains, and planes, and if they wish to
hitchhike will have to figure out some shipping and storing
system (I leave that to you-all, after all I can't be responsible
for *all* details).

How beautiful life would be. Somebody says "Let's go to
Aphganotropolis." And you say all right, snap the lid of your
footlocker shut (it should always be in perfect order as in the
Army), heist your pack, kiss your beloved, and go.

Think, also, of the grand celebrations attendant upon the
replacement of any article. You say, "I need a new pair of
tennis shoes." The crowd falls into a hush. Soon murmurs
begin, until finally you are surrounded by happy excited faces
all trying to tell you where you should buy your new tennis
shoes, how much you should pay, and so forth. Following this
outburst preparations are made for destroying the old tennis
shoes (by now quite worthless, beyond even the help of
GoodWill Angels). The destruction ceremony, of course, is the
occasion for the gravest incantations, dances, orgies, and the
like — virgins must be found and gently violated. . . . .
goodbye   must get back to work   write me

Lew

[P.S.] dint mail Jan 5 note cause no envelope — now have
one

8 February 1960

Ti Jean — I don't think I'll call mine "The Whole United States" either, it's too pretentious. I don't know what I'm writing about — just go along scene by scene — but I do know that it's not about the whole United States. Leo Keeler just had a fine piece of ass and is now going to walk around Portland with his girl. Anna (a little old lady) has died and everybody is nicely settled in a new place. Phil Whalen has already visited and a great building has been torn down to make a parking lot.

I think I'll call the book, "I, Leo."

Is it all right just to tell a story? I keep wondering why anybody would be interested in Leo. I don't know whether to write like an old river rat, or let Leo grow into an old river rat — I don't understand. Do you ever lose confidence? Then what do you do?

The trouble is I have been terribly depressed. My mother's little dog died horribly — distemper bug eating at its little nerve linings so it twitched and drooled and then died. She could hardly stand it, since for her the dog was all the company she had. My being here helped her a lot. Maybe her depression has rubbed off on me. It is getting a little better.

I have been reading tremendously: *Sons and Lovers* (reread), *Nausea, Sun Also Rises, Varieties of Religious Experience*, all of *Leaves of Grass* (for the first time, I never have been a real Whitman fan and even now am not really sent by him), also *Dharma Bums* (again), and a couple new Zen books, plus the sad life of Hart Crane. When I read this much I don't write real well or often, so now I'm meditating again (1 hr. upon arising) and we ought to get back into it.

I can't write as fast as you — maybe cause I can't type that fast. So if I get 5 feet on a good day it is about the limit. And lately I've only been doing about 10 feet a week. But this week have an absolute goal of 25 feet. This should get me nearly through school and into the insane part.

I got a message to try for a Guggenheim. Think I'll send them copies of the first third of this book and the plan, plus asking for letters from friends etc. This would be $2,500 for 1961 and I could stay in Japan, if we go there — or go there if we don't. Or both.

Mother is very poor because of bad management in Dec. All Dec. money was spent and all Jan. money by Xmas — that put us in the hole for Feb. so there isn't any dough to fix Willy (he needs $150 to get the charley horses out of him after the long bowl-game over the whole New Ninety States: intercepting miraculous passes and sweeping all ends and breaking his teeth in furious game-saving tackles etc.).

I am supposed to get my great poem *Wobbly Rock* published by Auerhahn Press as soon as they finish Whalen's big book. That will mean a trip to S.F., which I need, and all the fun of choosing type and handsetting it and generally balling around. I thought it would happen about now, but there have been snags in Whalen's book so maybe not till early March. Then I will arrive in S.F. the penniless bhikkhu, by bus, not trusting Willy — or rather I don't want to seriously break him apart.

I am trying to help Mom buy a house here in Reno. It is time consuming but fun. The point is she will have to have a lawsuit to get money out of an old trust, but then won't have rent to pay and will do better. She works way too hard for a lady near 60, but it keeps her mind off of things and she don't get too gloomy when working — but I want to help her get good use out of her $s and she is impractical and sad.

I think the best time for our huge trip into the woods will be late March, is that all right? What we do is take off into the mine and if we discover we can't live there very long then we stay a few weeks, or as it turns out. If, on the other hand, we like it we stay, or we can go into the mountains elsewhere or live a while in Nat'l Parks. There are thousands in Oregon and all are pretty. But the main thing is to try to set up the old Benton mine, catch huge fish, live well, and sit right on the very skin of this beautiful planet — having sloughed off all of Mansworld for a little while. I need it terribly.

Dark pines
White water
The sound is the same

And by late March I'll have my 1st 3rd done and on 11 x 8½
in duplicate for preselling and Guggenheim.
 How is yr. book going? Are moviemakers still delaying
On the Road? Did Burroughs come back with strange tales?
 I wrote Gary a long letter. Joanne is on the way. I dread
that meeting, though both will come out Buddhas because of
it even though the marriage will either never happen or last 5
months. What can you say? — The wheel turns — shall I
blow my breath upon the spokes? — Not while the driver
whips the ox!
 Thank you for instructions. Here's what I have in front of
this typewriter: (1) a photograph of a perfect lion looking right
at me (2) the inscription:

The look of the lion disdains all matter of opinion
. . . "the bay mare shames silliness out of me"

I miss you Buddha-the-red-face, Dancer . . .

                                                    Lew

Printed in the USA
CPSIA information can be obtained
at www.ICGtesting.com
JSHW082225140824
68134JS00015B/735

9 780912 516042